# Dressing fo...

## A Fresh Look at What Christians Wear in Church

## Dick Hines

Vice-Principal of North Thames Ministerial Training Course
and Lecturer at Oak Hill College, London

**GROVE BOOKS LIMITED**
RIDLEY HALL RD  CAMBRIDGE  CB3 9HU

# Contents

**Author's Note**

This booklet is not quite the same as other Grove Worship Booklets in that—rather than breaking much new ground—it has tended to review well-trodden paths. This seemed to be necessary in order to offer the guidance which many today are seeking on this subject. For his willingness to permit this approach the editor deserves my special thanks.

I also gladly offer thanks to members of the Group for the Renewal of Worship (GROW), and especially to Philip Tovey, for advice and critical comments. And likewise, to Nick Lyness and Clive Main—ordinands at Oak Hill College—for their helpful remarks after reading an early draft of this work.

Lastly I thank God for Jen, my wife—for her companionship, never-failing support and daily reassurance. Whatever is of value in this booklet I dedicate to her, with my love.

**The Cover Illustration** is by Peter Ashton

**First Impression** October 1996
**ISSN** 0144-1728
**ISBN** 1 85174 327 8

# 1
# *Introduction*

'What are the plans for Sunday evening?' I asked of the curate from my local parish church. I had been invited to preach. 'Should I bring my robes?' I knew that what was being arranged was an *'informal'* service and I had a feeling he might prefer the clergy to dispense with the usual black cassock, white surplice and black scarf. 'Oh no, no robes' he replied. 'We won't be bothering with robes. Just put your dog-collar on, and then whatever you feel comfortable in. Mind you,' he added, 'we did have one person walk out with a rather stony expression on his face last time we did it. I was a bit surprised really. I didn't expect it of him.'

Was the Church of England curate right to do as he did? Was the man who walked out of the service intolerant or did he have good reason for being upset? What principles should determine whether special dress is worn for worship— be it by Anglican ordained ministers or the ministers of other denominations, lay ministers, choir members, servers, vergers or whoever? Is it simply a matter of personal taste or is there more to it than that?

This booklet has been written with different kinds of people in mind. Firstly, anyone for whom the following sorts of questions have arisen: 'Where on earth does the idea of special dress for clergy in worship come from anyway? When and where did it all start? And why was it ever felt necessary for them to wear it in the first place?' For them I have attempted a simple and straightforward account which is necessarily brief but begins in the early pages of the Old Testament and passes through the New Testament before sketching in the background up to the present day (see chapters 2-4).

Secondly, I have in mind those who accept that down through the centuries the church has generally required of its leaders that they dress in special clothes at the time of worship, but who nevertheless seriously and sincerely question whether such a practice is appropriate for *today*. And, if it is defensible, on what basis? I have in mind those who are particularly concerned lest the image which the church projects is that of an anachronistic institution, stuck in the past, whose 'mumbo jumbo' and dressing up have no contemporary relevance. They, like many in our day and age, are image-conscious and are at pains to avoid putting unnecessary obstacles in the way of those they seek to reach with the good news of God's love for them as shown in Jesus Christ. For them I have explained the main reasons why some believe that ministers *should* be robed.

Thirdly, I have kept in mind the needs of those training for an ordained or authorized lay ministry, those who belong to robed choirs or who are vergers or servers, and any others who are required to wear special garments for public worship. They all might feel the need to reflect carefully on what their ministry will involve them in, and how they will respond to those who someday may challenge them about the matter.

But I have written with other people in mind too. To these Christians—the majority—this whole subject may seem an obscure matter which is a peculiar (even perverse) concern of ministers of a church and is, for all others, of no interest whatsoever. Paradoxically most of them would reckon it normal—indeed, quite enjoyable—to think carefully what they should wear when they go to some special occasion. How then should they dress when we gather for *worship*? Are there ways in which without realizing it we subtly influence—for better or for worse—each others' attitude and sense of occasion through what we wear when we gather? These and other questions are worth thinking about—if, that is, we have a proper sense of responsibility about what we do and how we do it when we gather for worship in the name of the Lord.

---

# 2
# *'With Dignity and Honour'*
# *Dressing for Worship in Ancient Israel*

The first hint from the Old Testament that it might matter what a person wears in the presence of God was when Moses—instructed by God—removed his sandals because he was standing on holy ground (Ex 3.5).[1] The detailed plans which God later gave to Moses about the tabernacle included specific directions about special garments—the work of a skilled craftsman—to be worn by those who would serve as high priest and priests. Both the high priest and the priests were to wear linen *undergarments*, a linen *tunic* and an *embroidered sash*. Priests were also to wear a linen *headband*.[2] Except on the Day of Atonement (Lev 16.3,4) the high priest was also required to wear the *robe of the ephod* over the tunic (from the robe's hem hung 'bells of pure gold' and decorative 'pomegranates'), an *ephod*, the *breastpiece* and linen *turban*.[3] Garments were consecrated for use by sprinkling with the blood of a sacrifice and anointing with special oil and were subsequently handed down through the generations.[4]

1  Some Christians today (eg in Ethiopia)—and of course Muslims too, throughout the world—remove their shoes for worship.
2  Ex 20.26; 29.4-9; 28.42; 39.27,28; Lev 16.4.
3  Ex 28.9f (cf 1 Sam 2.19; Ex 28.15-30; 29.6; 28.38).
4  Ex 29.21; 30.22; Lev 16.4,24; Ex 29.29-30; Nu 20.28.

Consecrated priests, however, were not the only ones to wear special robes for worship. King David arranged for Levites to be appointed as singers and musicians and each of them wore 'a robe of fine linen.' David himself is recorded as having worn a linen ephod on one important occasion though he appears not to have reverenced the ephod to quite the extent that Gideon did, thereby encouraging a new form of idolatrous practice.[5]

But why *were* special garments worn? Firstly, and quite simply, priests wore special garments because it was believed that God had commanded it through Moses. One reason that is specifically mentioned is that it was 'to give them [the priests] dignity and honour' (Ex 28.2, 40). But the whole system of approaching God through sacrifice and offerings, together with regulations governing ceremonial cleanliness, all served to highlight profound truths about God (his holiness) and about Israel (their sinfulness). Sacrifices were not so much brought by the Israelites, as given by God (Lev 18.11) to make atonement for themselves. The Israelites were to approach God on *his* terms not theirs. Thus a sense of the awesome perfection of God was communicated through the requirement to have all things used in worship to be ritually cleansed through sprinkling with blood.

Secondly, such garments distinguished the office and function of the individual or group concerned. There was a distinction between what the high priest wore on the Day of Atonement to enter the Holy of Holies, what other priests wore for the daily sacrifices, and what the Levites as singers and musicians wore. It would have been possible to see at a glance who was who and who did what.

Thirdly, there is a clear sense in which priests wore robes before God *on behalf* of Israel, in some kind of representative way. Certainly the community of faith had a tangible stake in or connection with the robes. They had actively participated in providing the garments since their free-will offerings (Ex 35.20-36.7) had been used by the skilled craftsmen Bezalel and Oholiab who manufactured them (Ex 35.34). The two engraved onyx stones carried one in each shoulder piece of the ephod, and the twelve precious stones carried in the fold of the breastpiece, were engraved with the names of the tribes of Israel and were the symbolic means by which all Israel was brought regularly '…as a memorial before the Lord' (Ex 28.12, 29). Moreover, the way in which Aaron and his sons conducted themselves and their ministry on behalf of Israel before the Lord was vital for the well-being of the community. Unkempt hair and torn robes could result not only in death for the scruffy priest but also in God's anger resting on the community as a whole.[6]

---

5   1 Chron 15.27, cf 1 Sam 2.28; Ju 8.27.
6   Ex 35.20-36.7; 28.12,29; Lev 10.6 cf 13.45.

# 3
## 'Clothe Yourselves With…Jesus Christ'[7]
### Early Customs

In complete contrast to the detailed regulations of the worship of Israel, very little instruction is given in the New Testament for ordering the worship of the disciples of Jesus. The apostles were not, of course, temple priests, and they soon understood that Jesus had inaugurated a *new* covenant through his self-sacrifice on the cross, thus ending the need for any further sacrifice for sin to be offered. And so the sacrificial system of the temple with its sacrificing priests dressed in their special garments was now obsolete. There is virtually nothing in the New Testament documents which may be legitimately regarded as a justification for anyone wearing special clothes when Christians gather for praise and prayer, or for the Lord's Supper. Perhaps the one exception we should note is the instruction of Paul regarding women's head covering. Paul regarded women prophesying or praying without their head covered (or 'veiled,' RSV) as dishonourable, though it is not clear precisely why. There is a hint in the text that others did not see eye to eye with Paul on this matter.[8]

There are some notable references, however, to clothing in general which clearly applied as much to the assembled church as to the dispersed church. It was the rich and powerful who were often sumptuously dressed and ostentatious in their lifestyle. These same people exploited the poor and powerless and neglected the needy around them. This alone would have been reason enough not to imitate them but the teaching of Jesus and his apostles would not have encouraged anyone to emulate them either. There was, after all, always the temptation to show partiality to the better-dressed person. Then again there was the ever-present temptation to use one's clothes to show off, which Jesus had warned his disciples about. Perhaps this was a temptation that Jesus had first-hand experience of since it would seem that he too wore a robe with fringes on, probably like the one the Pharisees wore.[9] We may assume that generally speaking the early Christians were poor rather than well-off. The apostles were often ill-clad, and some persecuted believers resorted to animal skins. What with this and the example of John the Baptist to follow, few Christians would have or could have dressed extravagantly. Notwithstanding this there are two specific instructions given about what was appropriate for reverent, chaste and submis-

---

**7** Rom 13.14.
**8** Lk 22.20; Heb 9.11, 23-28; 10.10,11; Rom 15.15,16; 1 Cor 11.4-16.
**9** Luke 8.44—The Greek word *kraspedon*, translated 'border' (RSV), should perhaps be translated 'tassel' or 'fringe.' It is the same word Jesus is recorded as using (Mt 23.5) to describe the fringes of the Pharisees' garments.

sive women to wear.[10] As in the Old Testament so also we find in the New Testament that the imagery of clothes and clothing is used in a metaphorical sense.[11]

But it was John's glimpse into heaven that was later to provide inspiration for what some Christians wore when gathered for worship. For John noted that the elders around the throne (Rev 4.4), the martyrs (Rev 6.11) and the great multitude (Rev 7.9) were all given white robes to wear, and some had golden crowns, others palm branches to carry. Thus dressed they would have resembled some of the angels (Rev 15.6) and possibly Jesus himself (Rev 1.13; cf Lk 9.29). At one point the cry of the great multitude includes an explanation of the white robes. These are part of the celebrations at the marriage supper of the Lamb in heaven. The white robes are '...fine linen, bright and pure' and represent the righteous deeds of the saints (Rev 19.6-9) and they contrast strongly with the clothes and finery lusted after by the inhabitants of 'Babylon' (Rev 18.16).

---

# 4
# *'Girded with a Shining Vesture'*[12]
# *Changing Habits*

The origins of special garments for Christian worship is by no means clear. However, in what follows below, in addition to a brief description of each garment, an account is also given of the generally accepted view regarding those most commonly worn now by ministers of the main Western traditions.[13] Some clergy attach a particular and symbolic meaning to their garments and may say a form of 'vesting prayer' as a devotional preparation whilst they dress for worship.[14] Official Roman Catholic documents give no explanation of any symbolism attached to Mass vestments other than the fact that they are intended to symbolize the function of each minister who wears them. In some traditions clerical dress is governed by canon (or church) law. Thus for Church of England

---

**10** Js 5.1-6; Lk 16.19; Mt 6.19-21, 25-34; Js 2.15; 2.1ff; Mt 23.5; 1 Cor 1.26-29; Js 2.5; Heb 11.37; Mt 11.8; 1 Tim 2.9ff; 1 Pet 3.3.
**11** Mt 22.11; Rom 13.12; Eph 6.13ff; Col 3.10,12,14; 1 Pet 5.5.
**12** A rubric in a liturgy attributed to Clement, Bishop of Rome (died c100 AD), directs a priest to begin the service 'girded with shining vesture.' Quoted in J Mayo, *A History of Ecclesiastical Dress* (London: Batsford, 1984) p 15.
**13** For a concise but useful account see 'Vestments' in J G Davies (ed), *A New Dictionary of Liturgy and Worship* (London: SCM, 1986).
**14** The text of some commonly used prayers is published by the Additional Curates' Society.

ministers Canon B8 directs what is to be worn, and for ministers of the Roman Catholic Church the *General Instruction of the Roman Missal* lists one of the requisites for celebrating mass as 'vestments.'[15]

## Vestments

The following are usually referred to as 'vestments' and are worn at the Eucharist (Mass or Holy Communion).[16]

The *Alb* is a full-length garment, usually made of cotton, and tied with a rope-type belt (girdle) at the waist. It derives from the undergarment of Roman citizens known as the *tunica alba* (the white tunic) and may be regarded as equivalent to the vest or shirt of the 3rd or 4th century. The *tunica*, though often a short garment, occurred also in a longer version—perhaps with narrow sleeves—and may have been belted at the waist. Some modern-style albs, known also as 'cassock albs,' are fashioned so as not to need a girdle and are in effect cassock (see below) and alb combined into one simple garment. In the Roman Catholic Church the alb is to be worn by ministers of every rank (bishops, priests, deacons and other ministers) and must cover all 'street clothing.' In the Church of England the canons permit an alb to be worn with (that is, over) a cassock by the celebrant or presiding priest at Holy Communion. In practice in the Church of England, in a place where albs are worn it is likely that all the clergy and their assistants would each wear an alb.

The *Amice* is a thin rectangular cotton scarf which is sometimes worn around the neck (Latin *amicio* 'I wrap round'). It is worn partly to cover ordinary clothes and also to help keep the neck of the alb clean. The amice derives from the neck cloth used in Roman times but was not in regular use as a liturgical garment until about the 10th century.

The *Dalmatic* is a more or less ornate broad-sleeved garment that may hang down to mid-thigh level, with a square-cut neck. It is worn without a girdle. In the Roman Catholic Church 'the dalmatic, worn over the alb and stole [see below] is the vestment proper to the deacon.'[17] In the Church of England some deacons wear a dalmatic on festive occasions but not during the penitential seasons of Lent and Advent. The dalmatic has developed from a particular form of the *tunica alba*, originally made of wool and from the region of Dalmatia. It became popular as a garment with ordinary citizens in Rome during the 2nd century.

---

**15** *The Canons of the Church of England: Canons Ecclesiastical promulged by the Convocations of Canterbury and York in 1964 and 1969 and by the General Synod of the Church of England from 1970* (London: CHP, Fifth Edition, 1993, with Second supplement, issued March 1996). See also Thomas C O'Brien (ed & trans), *The Documents on the Liturgy, 1963-1979: Conciliar, Papal and Curial Texts* (Collegeville: Liturgical Press, 1982) pp 523-525, paras 1687-1700.

**16** Obviously illustrations would have helped at this point but a telephone call to any good ecclesiastical outfitter should quickly procure glossy brochures with lots of helpful pictures.

**17** Thomas C O'Brien (ed & trans) *op cit*, p 524.

The *Stole* is a strip of material, about 4" wide, often of silken brocade, with fringed or tasselled ends and usually with a cross embroidered at each end and at the centre. In the Roman Catholic Church now 'The priest wears the stole around his neck and hanging down in front. The deacon wears it over his left shoulder and drawn across the chest to the right side where it is fastened.'[18] The stole is one of the vestments '...proper to the priest celebrant at Mass and other rites immediately connected with the Mass.'[19] In the Church of England a stole may be worn with cassock and surplice at the 'Occasional Offices' that is, the baptism or confirmation services, the marriage service or funeral service, and with cassock and alb at Holy Communion.

The modern stole owes its origins to the *orarium*, a strip of material originally worn by bishops (perhaps in imitation of secular dignitaries) to signify their authority. Certainly by the early 7th century it was given to some if not all clergy at their ordination but it was not widely termed the 'stole' in the West until late medieval times.[20] The stole as worn by a deacon has often been taken as a sign of being girded with a towel ready for 'foot washing' or lowly service—see John 13.3, where, of course, we read that Jesus tied the towel around his waist!

The *Chasuble* is a 'poncho' style garment with an opening for the head and tailored so as to provide for the arms of the priest to extend and hold books, for prayer and other actions during the Eucharist. It is derived from an outer garment or cloak (cf 1 Tim 4.13) of Roman times, known as the *paenula* (also known as the *casula*, Latin 'little house' or 'tent'). In the Roman Catholic Church 'the chasuble, worn over the alb and the stole, is the vestment proper to the priest celebrant at Mass and other rites immediately connected with the Mass.'[21] In the Church of England a chasuble as such is not mentioned in the canons but the phrase 'customary vestment' opens the way for the chasuble to be worn, as indeed it commonly is, over alb and stole during Holy Communion.

### Choir Habit

The following garments are not usually referred to as 'vestments' but rather as 'choir habit,' that is, garments for clergy when ministering in the chancel area or 'choir,' as opposed to the 'sanctuary' of a church. Those who regularly wear vestments for the Eucharist or a stole at the Occasional Offices might well wear choir habit for Morning and Evening Prayer or other occasions. Little or no symbolism attaches to most of these garments nor has a tradition of prayer equivalent to 'vesting prayers' developed.

A *Cassock* is a full-length garment with long narrow sleeves, usually worn

18  O'Brien *ibid.*
19  *Ibid*, p 524.
20  *Ibid*, p 23.
21  *Ibid*, p 524.

with a belt, and buttoned from head to foot. A cassock is often made of black material, especially for clergy, but occasionally—for others—of red, scarlet, blue or purple. Cassocks are worn by Anglican clergy, either under vestments or with a surplice as choir dress, and by others such as vergers, servers, Readers, choristers and organists. They are also worn by some but not all Methodist ministers. The cassock (as the cope) is possibly derived from the long outdoor cloak (the byrrus) which was in use in the 3rd century. The Council of Braga ordered the use of a cassock by all clergy in 572 AD.

The *Surplice* is a smock-like garment of white cotton or similar material usually worn over a cassock and (by clergy) with scarf or stole. A wide aperture is provided for the neck and the garment has wide full sleeves. Surplices are quite plain but a short form of the surplice known as the *Cotta* has a square neck line and may be trimmed with lace. Surplices are worn by Anglican clergy, Readers, servers, choristers and organists (perhaps with sleeves specially adapted to permit easy arm movement when conducting or playing). Surplices derive from the alb and may originally have been cut full to cover the bulky fur-lined cassocks of clergy in colder climes.

The *Scarf* (or, less commonly, 'tippet') is a long black accessory of silk-like material worn in the way a priest might wear a stole, sometimes referred to as a 'preaching scarf.' It is worn by bishops, priests and deacons of the Church of England. Readers in the Church of England may wear a mid-blue coloured scarf. The scarf probably derives from part of the cape section of the medieval university hood which hung down the front. Today's scarf and hood are therefore most probably separated parts of one original garment known as an *almuce*.

The academic *Hood* is a piece of fine cloth, usually black, in the form of (but never used as) a hood which hangs from the neck over the back of the shoulders. Hoods are usually lined with coloured silk or silk-like material and are worn as part of choir dress by university and other graduate clergy of the Church of England. Hoods originate from the medieval university hood or almuce and no symbolism attaches to them as such. But the colour of the silk denotes the institution or university which conferred the award or degree.

The *Cope* is a long full cloak, often made of silk brocade or velvet, secured high across the chest with a clasp (or 'morse') and with a 'hood' hanging part way down the back. Copes are particularly common on festive occasions and in cathedrals or abbey churches. The origin of the cope is disputed but it seems to have come either from the *byrrus*, a brown cloak or cape with a hood worn by northern barbarian tribes who eventually overcame the Romans, or from the *paenula*, and thus shares a common ancestry with the chasuble. It is not difficult to imagine how an outer cloak such as this would be much appreciated in cold climes and in winter.

The *Gown* (the Geneva or preaching gown) is a black garment, open at the front, with wide bell-shaped sleeves. It was adopted by John Calvin—hence the name Geneva gown—in the 16th century and since then has been generally preferred by ministers of the Reformed tradition. Variations of the Geneva gown are worn by Baptist and Presbyterian ministers and Anglican vergers. Like the hood and scarf its origins are from the academic dress of medieval times.

*Bands* (known also as 'preaching bands' or 'Geneva bands') are two strips of white linen material, 6-8" long, which hang from the collar below the chin. Some Anglican clergy wear bands with choir dress. They are also often worn by Methodist, URC or Presbyterian ministers together with the gown. Bands were adopted as conventional dress by the legal and clerical profession in the 17th and 18th century

Other garments, which are worn by Anglican bishops include the *Rochet*—a white cotton garment, worn over the cassock, and derived from the alb but with rather fuller sleeves, gathered at the wrists. The *Chimere*—a full-length garment, without sleeves, made of silky or satin material usually in scarlet but sometimes in black—is worn over the rochet and cassock and with a scarf and pectoral cross. The *Mitre* is worn by Roman Catholic and most Anglican bishops together with their episcopal garments. It is a crown-like hat, the top part of which rises up to two distinct points, one at the front and one at the back. Since the mitre can be regarded (with a little stretch of the imagination) as having the appearance of two giant flames of fire a tradition has grown up which associates the mitre and its wearer with the descent of the Holy Spirit in Pentecostal fire and power.

# 5
## Dressing for Worship Today: Origins, Continuity and Unity

We must conclude that in the first century most people (if not everyone)—leaders, preachers, congregations—wore everyday clothes for worship. But given the customs that have developed since, what can be said in favour of using the kind of garments decribed above, in our day and age? In this and succeeding chapters we will examine some of the reasons most often given.

*Origins and Continuity*
  In the realm of human society there is a universal tendency to adopt particular or special clothes for significant and ceremonial occasions. As Gilbert Cope has expressed it:

'Psychologically, it seems that people who engage in the corporate performance of ritual desire that some, if not all, of the participants should wear special clothing.'[22]

Any institution which exists long enough tends to adopt some kind of distinctive dress by which members of that institution may be identified, even if that dress is no more than a neck tie with a particular kind of badge on it. Such dress will not be subject to regular change and adaptation, and neither would its members wish it so. For example, inside the Vatican City in Rome as one approaches St Peter's Basilica, one can still see the bright costumes (designed by Michelangelo) of the Swiss Guards who for centuries and by tradition have always been loyal and trustworthy servants of the papacy. Such people in their distinctive costume are a sign of an enduring institution. Of course there is a certain sense in which they look ridiculous when analysed in the cold light of day. But we do not usually think this way. Rather, most of us accept, enjoy, and feel somewhat reassured about what they represent of the stability and endurance of the institution.
  During the 4th and 5th centuries the prevalent Roman style of dress gradually fell into disuse for everyday life—fashions changed then as they do now—and was replaced by styles which owed more to their new barbarian rulers. However, in the Christian church, now publicly recognized by the state, its own publicly recognized (ordained) leaders—bishops, priests and deacons—tended

22 See the article by Cope 'Vestments' in J G Davies, *op cit*, p 537.

to retain the Roman style of dress, certainly for the formal public gatherings in the basilicas and churches. Why did they do this? No doubt it was an attempt to express continuity with the past order of things, to express a certain 'business as usual' or 'things around may change but the church is still here' kind of message, and no doubt the message was to themselves as much as to society at large. Perhaps most importantly they sought to convey the conviction—again, to themselves as much as to others—that they were continuing true to the faith and practice which they had inherited from the apostles and from Jesus Christ himself. Of course the garments (and especially their style) were not significant in and of themselves. The significance lay in their continuity with what went before. Michael Perham, with special reference to the Eucharist, reiterated the validity of the 'continuity' factor above the 'origins' factor as far as special garments for worship today is concerned. For us modern-day Christians as well the significance of special garments

> '...lies more in their historical continuity in Western Christendom than in their precise origins...the continuity has been there, and their use today is one way of rooting what we do in the Eucharist with what the church has always done.'[23]

Thus the identity, continuity and endurance of the church as the human institution comprising the disciples of Jesus Christ and the inheritors of the apostolic faith can be given tangible and outward expression through the dress of its clerical leaders.

## Unity

The rubrics of the first liturgies in English, compiled largely by the reforming Archbishop Thomas Cranmer, provide evidence that the uniformity of liturgical forms which he desired for the Church of England was to be complemented by a uniformity of clerical vesture. These days, however, it is not so since a wide diversity of dress is legally permitted. Thus it cannot be said confidently that, as far as the Church of England is concerned, the robes of the ministers serve to any great extent to express unity or any sense of coherence within the denomination.

Certainly the link of identity between what ministers wear and what the church or some branch of it believes is indisputable and Perham was quick to mention this too. It is, he acknowledges

> '...the precise reason why some have wanted to abandon the use of the traditional eucharistic vestments of Western Christianity. They would want to

---

**23** M Perham, *Lively Sacrifice: The Eucharist in the Church of England Today* (London, SPCK, 1992) p 82.

say that what the church did at the Reformation was to make a break with medieval doctrine, and the vestments were part of the way that doctrine was expressed.'[24]

For a long time now in the Church of England the garments clergy wear (or decline to wear) have been a clue to their eucharistic theology. Thus, in the 'Vacancies' columns of the church press, churches are often described in ways that include reference to what the ministers wear for worship. This may well be a code for what the priest is likely to believe about the Eucharist and other services.

All this is perhaps a source of amusement to those from churches of other denominations where a simple black gown or an ordinary lounge suit is the order of the day. But their practice only serves to make this tragic point more forcefully—that in our present situation the issue of ministers' robes can highlight and reinforce differences among Christians as much as they express any unity in and continuity from common origin. As Cope summed it up:

'...vestments (themselves derived from ordinary clothing) have become badges of party in ecclesiastical conflicts.'[25]

---

6

# Office and Function

### Uniforms Act as Signs

Clerical garments function as a kind of uniform. They tell you very little about the person wearing them, but then they are not meant to. Instead they indicate—at least to those who know the code—the authorization given and the responsibilities held by the wearer and perhaps about the particular role or function he or she performs. Thus at a Roman Catholic Mass or perhaps in an Anglican Communion service the president (a bishop or presbyter) can be identified as the one wearing the alb, stole and chasuble. A deacon could be recognized by the presence of a stole tied across the chest and fastened at the side or perhaps by the dalmatic which is being worn.

Not only does dress identify a person's function and office in the *local* cel-

24 Perham *op cit*, pp 82-83.
25 Cope, *op cit*, p 537.

ebration but it serves also as a kind of sign of the way in which the ministerial order of the *wider* church is represented at the local level. The uniform of a presbyter (priest) in the Church of England is basically the same uniform as a presbyter (priest) in the Episcopal Church of the USA, the Church of New Zealand or anywhere else throughout the Anglican communion. Indeed if alb, stole and chasuble are worn by the presbyter who is president at the Eucharist then the uniform is more or less the same throughout much of the worldwide Christian church

But *should* a 'uniform'—the word itself speaks volumes about the function of such clothes—be necessary *'in church'*? Will not most of the people know who the president is anyway? Would it not soon become obvious, in so far as it was necessary to know at all? But this is to regard the phenomenon of wearing special clothes for special functions as *entirely* functional; it is not as simple as that. In so many different walks of life certain individuals who perform different functions and have different responsibilities also dress differently. They use the colour, shape and design of their clothing, together with other insignia, to show who they are and what they do. Men and women from widely divergent ethnic, cultural and religious backgrounds use clothing in this way as a part of an integrated and complex system of non-verbal communication. This phenomenon is widespread and is not restricted to certain sections of the Christian church in the West. To deny this is to deny a basic fact about what it means to be human.

### A Uniform Sets a Person Apart in Different Ways

A uniform diverts unnecessary attention away from the individual who wears it to the authority and meaning that the uniform signifies and represents. But is such depersonalization required in the church? At the least a uniform reminds wearer and observer alike that the minister does not hold him or herself up as the final authority to preach or exercise the particular pastoral role of presiding at and leading worship. In the Church of England no person takes it upon him or herself and decides that he or she will become a deacon, priest or bishop. Those who have the right to wear the uniform were first tested and found to be duly called by God to their ministry; they publicly committed themselves to certain specific beliefs about God and the Holy Scriptures. Behind the public façade of the role in leading worship Sunday by Sunday should be the commitment to a life of prayer, study and holiness for the sake of the gospel in the parish where such people serve. All ordained ministers should reflect soberly as they don their clerical garb for a church service. For in so doing they make a public statement about the high calling which by God's grace they have embraced.

'If clerical robes are not to be worn then what should be worn instead?' A friend who lives in East London was once told that when she is up front leading worship she should try to wear clothes with which members of her congregation

15

can identify. This leaves my friend with the challenge of deciding *which* members of her congregation she should dress to please. Should she wear jeans, a T-shirt and a pair of trainers for the sake of the youngsters who attend? Or should she perhaps choose a *sari* so that those Christian women of Asian origin who attend on Sunday morning can identify with her? Yet again, perhaps it should be a smart suit for those who have always thought it right to put on their 'Sunday best' to go to church. The point is a simple but important one. Arguably the wearing of a uniform sets ministers somewhat apart so that they are not seen as identifying with any particular section of a congregation or fellowship and at the same time enables everyone in the congregation, whatever their background or social status, whatever they have chosen (or have the money to afford) in the way of dress for church service, to be able to identify the minister(s) as ministering as much to them as to anyone else.

---

# 7

# *Occasion and Season*

Some of the sayings we use in conversation, often picked up from the news media, indicate the importance of the way we dress as part of our total human experience. Ambitious and get-ahead men and (more often) women are accused of 'power dressing' as they seek to convey a sense of energy and drive by their choice of clothes for work. A person who looks particularly stunning—usually said of a woman—is 'dressed to kill.' And there's no one quite so sad as the person who is 'All dressed up but with nowhere to go'! Clothes are also part of the way we celebrate special occasions. A wedding, an anniversary or a celebratory meal—for those who can afford it—is an opportunity for a new outfit. It is when teenagers first become self-aware in this regard that their parents' problems really begin. It is then that they crave the latest fashion clothes in order to dress like their friends.

Most of us do not spend our time analysing what we look at and the way it affects us. We do not need to. Without thinking about it we recognize instantly a person dressed up for a posh event or the bride on her way to the wedding. We can usually tell if a person is expecting good weather or rain and if they are at leisure or on business. Clothes signal certain bits of information to us while we are hardly aware of it. What we wear influences our response to one another more than we imagine. Advertisers and public relations experts are only too aware of this.

The effect which dress style has on us does not suddenly stop the moment we walk into church. It is precisely because we do not cease to be human—to be sensory creatures with eyes and aesthetic sensibilities—that the same dynamic forces continue to make their impact upon us. In some traditions the sight of the clergy in vestments serves as a reminder of what the congregation has gathered for. As the vested clergy enter the church the congregation is prompted to recall (albeit not always in a strikingly conscious way) that their gathering is not for relaxation, or for informal chat, or for letting their hair down. This occasion now, with their representatives—those presiding and leading the assembly on their behalf—dressed as they are, is the occasion for full attention to the Lord whose command they obey by celebrating the Eucharist. They have been gently reminded in a nonverbal way of what they are about. They are now to try and give full attention to singing God's praises, listening carefully to his Word and to praying with devotion and sincerity.

*Colour, Season and Mood*

In the early centuries of the Christian church it would seem that the only colour that had any particular significance was white (see chapter 3 above). There is evidence, however, that in Jerusalem in the twelfth century different coloured vestments were worn at different stages of the celebration of the important festival of Christmas. In the early thirteenth century Pope Innocent III proposed using white vestments for festivals, red vestments on days when martyrs were commemorated, black for penitential and green on all other non-festive or 'ferial' occasions.

The use of coloured vestments in the Church of England, though based on the Roman scheme of 1570, was not at all widespread until the impact of the Anglo-Catholic revival during the second half of the nineteenth century. Until then cassock, surplice, academic hood and black tippet (or scarf) were worn on all occasions. The *ASB* offers guidance concerning the appropriate coloured vestments to be worn.

And so it is that as the regular on-going life of the Christian church proceeds, with its different 'high days and holidays,' change and contrast punctuates the annual cycle. To note that the clergy and others are now wearing purple or violet-coloured vestments whereas last week they were wearing green vestments serves to remind the congregation that this week is the first Sunday in Advent (or perhaps Lent). In this way vestments act together with other things—music, lights, flowers for example—as part of a larger and more complex procedure of establishing the context and setting in which the assembly gathers for worship.

The colour of vestments thus helps to express the mood of particular occasions. At the great festivals—Christmas, the Epiphany and Easter—white and/or gold vestments are worn and these may contribute wonderfully to the overall mood of celebration and rejoicing which befits these occasions. But things

17

can change over time. For example, it is customary in some traditions today for purple or even black vestments to be worn at times of grief and sorrow such as a funeral service. The custom at Christian funerals in the early centuries was for those present to wear white garments. White, as the colour of celebration and joy, was deemed appropriate since a Christian's death is the gateway to eternity with Christ.

What, we may wonder, do the 'exteriors' of those in the congregation where we gather each week—the way they dress and so present themselves to you in public—tell you about their 'interiors'—their attitude and mood as they come to church? In this connection the custom of turning up at church in 'Sunday best' is worth considering. Doubtless those who live in suburban parts of the United Kingdom would regard this practice as outdated, for typically it would seem that these days people in such parts dress *down* for church. For those who for work purposes wear a suit and/or tie all week the chance to wear an open-neck shirt and casual trousers or jeans brings much welcome relief. And so gathering for worship each week is done in a relaxed kind of a way, rather in the same way that the same people might have gone out for a meal the night before. In rural areas however, although there have been changes along the lines of what has been described for suburbia, the tendency remains for people to dress *up* for church, for example a tie and jacket or perhaps a suit for men and a smart-ish dress or skirt and blouse for women. Generally speaking the approach is slightly more formal and perhaps just a little less relaxed. The question is, given that what each of us wears has some kind of effect upon others and *vice versa*, is it possible that our general approach to worship—our attentiveness in prayer, even our attitude perhaps towards God himself—is subtly affected, for better or for worse, by the clothes we wear?

# 8
# *Reverence and Beauty*

What part, if any, might the beauty of fabric texture, design and style of garments, colour and decorative embroidery have in contributing something valid to the worship of God? What part could they play, if any, in enhancing the dignity and reverence of our gatherings for worship?[26]

The *General Instruction on the Roman Missal* explains that the special garments or vestments worn by different ministers serve not only to signify the special role which each person has in the rite but they also 'make the ceremonies beautiful and solemn.' On the question of the attractiveness of liturgical garments the *Instruction* continues:

'The beauty and dignity of liturgical vestments is to be sought in the excellence of their material and the elegance of their cut, rather than in the abundance of adventitious ornamentation. Any images, symbols or figures employed in decorating vestments should be sacred in character and exclude anything inappropriate.'[27]

The overriding concern of the contemporary Roman Catholic Church, as far as its furnishings and vestments are concerned, is that the aim should always be 'to combine a noble simplicity with immaculate cleanliness.'[28]

Such detailed considerations of special garments for worship—though no doubt of special interest to some—will seem alien to many others. But it would be a mistake to think that 'low church' evangelicals have never bothered themselves with such things. One of the immediate results of the second National Evangelical Anglican Congress, held at Nottingham under the chairmanship of John Stott in April 1977, was the publication of *The Nottingham Statement*—an official corporate reaction to study materials which had been circulated and were then studied and discussed both before and during the Congress. It may

---

26 In the Roman Catholic *Constitution on the Sacred Liturgy* a separate chapter (chap VII) is devoted to the subject of 'sacred art and sacred furnishings.' Here in the introductory paragraph the conviction is implicit that finely made garments or vestments might enhance and even stimulate the worship and praise of God: 'The fine arts are rightly classed among the noblest activities of man's genius; this is especially true of religious art and of its highest manifestation, sacred art [directed towards specific use in worship]. Of their nature the arts are directed toward expressing in some way the infinite beauty of God in works made by human hands. Their dedication to the increase of God's praise and of his glory is more complete, the more exclusively they are devoted to turning men's minds devoutly toward God.' (p 34).
27 *Ibid*, p 197.
28 *Ibid*, p 198.

come as something of a surprise for some to discover that nearly twenty years ago more than 2000 leading evangelicals agreed to:

'...commend experimentation with...[amongst other things] colour, furnishings and setting to heighten the awareness of God's people in true worship.'[29]

The *Statement* nowhere makes specific mention of clerical robes; but in the section quoted above it is clear that cautious encouragement and implicit approval were offered to the idea that our general surroundings might have something useful and valid to contribute to the overall experience of congregational worship.

---

9

# Questions and Answers

The subject of dress in worship is hardly 'a Gospel issue' and any discussion of it must maintain a proper sense of perspective. Nevertheless as part of a complex anthropological, sociological, doctrinal and ecclesiastical phenomenon the subject continues to rouse strong feelings. The chapters above have reviewed the subject all too briefly. What follows is the author's equally brief answers to some of the pertinent questions he is often asked.

*What have special garments for the clergy to do with a true reverence and worship of God?*
   In one important sense clerical garments have nothing to do with true worship. True worship of God is—in David Peterson's words—'...a lifestyle of reverent obedience' rather than a dressing up in 'sacred' garb. As Peterson goes on to add:

'When Christians imply that reverence is essentially a matter of one's demeanour in church services, they show little understanding of the Bible's teaching on this subject!'[30]

Nevertheless Christians are not naked spirits but as human beings they can demonstrate inner heart-attitudes and convictions not only by posture and gesture—for which there is ample biblical precedent—but also by the way they

---

29 *The Nottingham Statement* (Falcon, 1977) para F3, p 24.
30 D Peterson, *Engaging with God: A Biblical Theology of Worship* (Leicester: Apollos, 1992) p 73.

dress. Perhaps they can show something of their reverence for God as the Creator of beauty and human aesthetic appreciation by giving creative and responsible thought and attention to what they wear. What more appropriate way is there to celebrate all that God's word teaches us of him as Creator of all things (as well as Redeemer of his people) than by being imaginative and creative in our choice of clothes generally—including our choices about clerical liturgical garments?

### Are some clergy required by Church law to use certain forms of dress?

In some traditions church laws certainly exist but individual interpretations of the nature and purpose of church law result in widely differing practices. The issue of dress then often leads into concerns over integrity. Some regard the Church of England's canons as 'norms' which need not be observed when prior evangelistic, sociological and even economic imperatives prevail. It is worth noting here that since a recent revision of Canon B8 ministers are no longer required to robe for Morning and Evening Prayer on weekdays and the wearing of surplice or alb with scarf or stole is only 'normally' required on Sundays. However the wearing of robes is still required ('shall wear') at all times for the Holy Communion, a requirement which at least one bishop regards as having been a 'dead letter' from the moment of implementation.[31] It is interesting to note that in many places 'low church' clergy will still robe for Holy Communion if for no other services.

But in the Church of England an ordained minister is not permitted to '...change the form of vesture used in a church or chapel in which he officiates unless he has ascertained by consultation with the parochial church council that such changes will be acceptable.'[32] Clergy should perhaps seize upon opportunities that are given them to explain the kinds of issues raised in this booklet. Then they and their church councils would be able to make informed and responsible decisions rather than deciding on the basis of ignorance or prejudice.

### Should it not be left to the individual minister to choose what, if any, special garments he or she wears for worship?

In some church traditions this is in fact the case and ministers are under no obligation to dress in a particular way. Yet in such traditions a conventional dress code often prevails. But in all traditions the temptation to 'individualism' is ever present and so we return again to the issues discussed above concerning uniform. These days the variety of designs which are available on personalized scarves rivals the infinite number of patterns which are available on traditional stoles. No doubt the creativity of designers and embroiderers is a source of delight and praise to God. But the choice of design can so easily deviate from

---

31 See comments by Bishop Colin Buchanan in *News of Liturgy*, April 1994, p 3.
32 Canon B8.2.

normal Christian symbolism which is recognizable, helpful and acceptable. The choice of design for scarves as for stoles should be made with care and should avoid the idiosyncratic and the abstruse.

### Are not ministers right to follow their conscience when important doctrinal issues are at stake?

As we have seen, both wearing special garments for worship and not wearing special garments for worship sends signals about a number of things, including doctrinal convictions. The decision whether or not to wear *vestments* is one which many Church of England men and women, nurtured within the 'evangelical' tradition, are having to make as increasingly they have opportunities to take up pastoral charge in a parish with a different ecclesiastical tradition. Those who have chosen to wear vestments may, for the sake of conscience, take refuge in the canons that:

> 'The Church of England does not attach any particular doctrinal significance to the diversities of vesture permitted…and the vesture worn by the minister…is not to be understood as implying any doctrines other than those now contained in the formularies of the Church of England.'[33]

Thus if a minister is content to minister in the Church of England and abide by its formularies then he or she, wearing any of the robes or vestments permitted by canon is not, officially at least, contributing to doctrinal deviation. But such ministers must be aware of the norms of the Roman Catholic Church, referred to above, and so of the traditional and indispensable 'catholic' connection between the wearing of certain vestments and a proper (that is, lawful) celebration of the Mass. If it is claimed that we have moved on from the days when the wearing of, say, a stole was a live issue, the fact remains that for some Christians the matter is of great symbolic importance and the passion with which many feel it right to make the point ought not to be underestimated. People still walk out of church in some distress as much over what an incumbent opts to wear as what he or she chooses not to wear.

### Why have many ministers opted for wearing the white cassock alb?

It might be simply that they cost a great deal less than a cassock, they are easily put on and taken off, and can be carried around without difficulty. They are simple and straightforward; they can be worn with or without a coloured scarf (a black scarf would not 'go') or with a stole; and they represent a return to the earliest garment ever worn by ministers or their assistants. One commenta-

---

**33** Canon B8.1. Note: '…no *particular* doctrinal significance' [my italics], and not '…no doctrinal significance,' as Perham (*op cit*, p 83) has it, is attached to the diversity of vesture permitted by this canon.

tor has spoken enthusiastically about cassock albs:
'It is easy to imagine that such new garments would be perfectly acceptable to most Protestants and, thus, it would be possible to use a vestment as an aid to Christian unity rather than as a badge of division.'[34]

*Don't decisions about whether to wear robes or not depend a lot on the circumstances and setting of worship?*
It is difficult and unnecessary to counter this point but inevitably opinions do vary. Colin Buchanan is surely right when he points out that

'...a cathedral rite, with a robed choir, choirmaster and organist, and a stately procession and formal pattern of seating, provides one scenario, and a noisy family communion in a dual-purpose building on a housing estate provides another. Robes feel to a president more and more odd, the closer he or she is placed physically to the congregation, till in a circle in a home group they reach the nadir of aesthetic defensibility.'[35]

*Why do some clergy use robes that look so scruffy and tatty?*
Whenever robes are worn by clergy, servers, choir or anyone else it is imperative that they be kept clean and as fresh as possible. An area dean once explained how 'tattiness' gave him cause for concern. He complained about 'the candle grease, filthy vestments, and altar furnishings' in one church he had oversight of. No doubt he would also have objected to ill-fitting garments, especially those that are far too short, and to unsuitable footwear. Brown shoes with black cassocks do not go well; they have been known to give serious offence at funerals, occasionally having been taken by mourners as a sign of disrespect for the deceased. Trainers seem not to go well with any kind of liturgical garment!

*Why should only the clergy have special dress for worship? Aren't there ways in which the congregation can share in this?*
In an Orthodox Jewish synagogue not only the Rabbi but *all* males over the age of 12 years wear a prayer shawl or *talith*. In these same synagogues both men and women cover their heads. As we have already noted there are Christian churches too where not only the ministers but indeed the whole congregation wears special clothes. Members of some black Pentecostal churches all wear a long white garment, an obvious allusion to the dress of the redeemed seen in heaven by John and recorded in Revelation (Rev 7.9). There is a strong sense then for these Pentecostalists, as signalled by their clothing, that *all* Christian people—not only their ministers—are set apart for the service and worship of God.
To this day a custom survives whereby those to be baptized as infants are

**34** Davies, *op cit*, p 539.
**35** In Davies, *ibid*, p 4.

brought to the church in their white 'christening' gown. In the 4th century all those who had just been baptized were immediately clothed in a white garment and head dress which was then worn at the Easter Eucharist and at all other services throughout the week. Just as priests of Old Testament times wore a white turban on their head so too, it was argued, it is appropriate for Christians to receive some sign of priesthood at their baptism, since they share a common priesthood as the people of God (1 Pet 2.9).

We may yet see something of a revival of such customs now that the Church of England's Liturgical Commission has drafted revised rites for baptism that include the opportunity for those just baptized to be clothed in a white robe. Any argument in support of *all* Christians wearing special clothes as signs of their having been set apart for the service of God could do no better than to begin with careful reflection upon the meaning of baptism.

But there are other ways in which the whole *congregation*, from the point of view of dress, can participate more fully in the celebration of festivals and special occasions. At Remembrancetide many people participate by wearing the red poppy and some congregations have made serious attempts to encourage its members to participate in the festive spirit of important occasions by suggesting that (if possible) everyone wears an item of white clothing on Easter Day and of red clothing on Pentecost Sunday.[36] Perhaps in place of items of clothing a rosette or badge could be worn instead but the overall effect of making the extra effort offers a more total experience of participation in the celebrations.

It is obvious that such an approach would have particular appeal for children. But that could easily be an excuse for adults to avoid the issue about the thoughtfulness and sense of anticipation with which we approach our Sunday gatherings. Just occasionally to have to think about what one will wear on these particularly special occasions may cause us to reflect more carefully on just what it is that will be celebrated and so it could help raise the level of expectation about the whole event. A congregation might even come *eagerly* to church on such occasions!

*How can I help keep the issue about dress for worship in proper perspective?*
We must respect those who think differently from us about such secondary matters. And we must all learn to pray from the heart the words of a well-known hymn:

> 'Let holy charity mine outward vesture be
> and lowliness become my inner clothing.'

---

**36** See T Lloyd, *Ceremonial in Worship* (Grove Worship Series No 75, Nottingham: Grove Books, 1981) p 14.